Bead Crochet Jewelry

Tools, Tips, and 15 Beautiful Projects

Linda Lehman

with

Shelley Grant

Schiffer Publishing Ltd

4880 Lower Valley Road, Atglen, PA 19310 USA

Library of Congress Cataloging-in-Publication Data

Lehman, Linda.
  Bead crochet jewelry: tools, tips, and 15 beautiful
projects / by Linda Lehman with Shelley Grant.
      p. cm.
  ISBN 0-7643-2023-8 (pbk.)
  1. Beadwork. 2. Crocheting. I. Grant, Shelley. II. Title.
TT860 .L45 2004
745.58'2—dc22
                          2003027129

Designed by Mark David Bowyer
Type set in Zurich Blk BT / Zurich BT

ISBN: 0-7643-2023-8
Printed in China

Published by Schiffer Publishing Ltd.
4880 Lower Valley Road
Atglen, PA 19310
Phone: (610) 593-1777; Fax: (610) 593-2002
E-mail: Info@schifferbooks.com

For the largest selection of fine reference books on this
and related subjects, please visit our web site at
www.schifferbooks.com
We are always looking for people to write books on new
and related subjects. If you have an idea for a book
please contact us at the above address.

This book may be purchased from the publisher.
Include $3.95 for shipping.
Please try your bookstore first.
You may write for a free catalog.

In Europe, Schiffer books are distributed by
Bushwood Books
6 Marksbury Ave.
Kew Gardens
Surrey TW9 4JF England
Phone: 44 (0) 20 8392-8585; Fax: 44 (0) 20 8392-9876
E-mail: info@bushwoodbooks.co.uk
Free postage in the U.K., Europe; air mail at cost.

Table of Contents

Tools of the Trade

There are three basic tools needed for every type of bead crochet. They are obvious; yarn, beads, and hooks. Less obvious are all the ways in which they interrelate. So let's start with the basics, the tools.

Yarn

An interesting note to begin: You can literally crochet anything, from dental floss to wire. I'm telling you this because, after reading what materials I like the best (and why), you may find something else you'd like to try. If a yarn isn't listed in this section, don't let that stop you from trying it, but I'll give you a couple of pointers on how to "rule out" certain materials in an effort to save you both time and trouble.

Many bead crocheters are fond of the non-natural fibers, such as bonded nylon or polyester (thread). I prefer the natural fibers. They tend to have a better "hand," as it is called. They handle better, are easier on your skin, and often increase your speed. They tend to have a bit of elasticity, which will allow you to relax a bit more when you crochet, making you less likely to incur injuries. Crochet cotton is also stiffer than the top stitch thread that is popular, enabling you to make a larger tube if you want to. If you find that you are not comfortable with the natural fibers described here, try the synthetics, and see if you like them better.

Cottons. There are many types of cotton crochet yarns available. Every time you venture into a craft store, you'll see shelves full of them. Many of them are not well-suited to "bead crochet." The heavily twisted (or multiple ply) cottons tend to be the best. The reason for this is simple: As you crochet, the beads run up and down the cotton many times. If the cotton has the bare minimum number of strands plied together, or is not heavily "corded" (twisted), the cotton may either "fuzz-up" or fray. The cottons listed below have all been tried, and have yielded excellent results. (If you have trouble finding any of them, check the "Resources" section in the back of this book.) Crochet cotton is generally sold by the ball and comes in various weights. The weights that lend themselves easily to bead crochet range from #5 weight to #30 weight. In some cases, you may decide you need a particularly thin yarn. Some of these cottons are also sold in both #50 and #80 weight, which would accommodate those special projects. The #50 and #80 cottons are very difficult to work with, so pick those projects with that in mind.

Opera. Opera is a very good crochet cotton that is available in sizes #5, #10, and #20. (It is also available in size #30, but with virtually no color selection.) Opera is one of the few good crochet cottons that is available in size #5.

Cébélia®. Cébélia® is an excellent crochet cotton made by DMC, and is widely distributed. It comes in a broad range of colors, with many available in sizes #10, #20, and #30. The #30 weight is equivalent to the polyester top stitch thread often used by bead crocheters. The #20 weight is equivalent to #8 "Perle" cotton, which is another material popular with bead crocheters.

Presencia. This yarn is perhaps the very best that I have used, but at the time of this writing is available only in white and ecru in size #30.

Flora. Flora is a very nice cotton that is offered in terrific colors, but at the time of this writing is available in this country only in sizes #10, #20, and #50.

Perle cotton. There are several companies that manufacture Perle cotton. The sizing is numbered differently than other crochet cottons. The #8 Perle cotton is roughly equivalent to a #20 weight crochet cotton, and a #12 Perle cotton is roughly equivalent to a #30 weight crochet cotton. It is slightly softer than the other cottons listed above. It is also not twisted as tightly, and, therefore, it is easy to "split" the yarn. On the positive side, it comes in well over 100 colors, and on small enough balls to allow you to have a good stock on hand without investing a lot of money.

Silks. There is a smaller range of silks available to bead crocheters. In my opinion, the best one available is Gudebrod. It comes in a wide assortment of colors and sizes. It handles beautifully, and wears well.

The sizes range from FFF, which is the largest size, to D, which is the smallest size that is available in a variety of colors.

Cotton versus silk. Size E silk is equivalent to #20 weight cotton, and D is equivalent to #30 weight cotton. Because silk is not as stiff as cotton, you may wish to use one size heavier weight in silk than in cotton. In other words, if you are particularly fond of using #30 weight cotton, you may wish to try size E silk to see if you like it before trying to use size D.

How do you know which material to use? In the broadest sense, use the material that is most comfortable for you whenever possible. Cotton will yield a slightly stiffer "tube." Silk has a more fluid feel and a greater "drape." If you are using large seed beads (such as size 6), you may want the added strength of cotton. If you are crocheting small pearls or gemstones, you may want the softness and fluidity of silk. A lot of this can be lumped under "rules of thumb," but, with just a few exceptions, it comes down to a personal preference. For example, if you want a beaded bag that can be used for everyday wear, you probably want to stick to cotton.

If you are wandering through a store and spot a yarn that you think you might like to use, and don't know if it would work, try this. Take a strand of the yarn between your fingers and rub your fingers up and down it several times. Does it seem to retain its finish, or does it get a little fuzzy? If the yarn fuzzes up during your test, don't bother. You'll have a very "linty" tube. If not, buy it, take it home, and string a foot or two of beads on it. Then make a swatch. See how you like it the next day.

Hooks

There are three manufacturers of crochet hooks that are widely distributed: Susan Bates, Boye/Wright, and Clover. The Susan Bates hooks generally have a sharper nose than the Boye/Wright hooks, while the Boye/Wright hooks tend to have a wider shaft than the Susan Bates hooks. Clover makes plastic and wood hooks in several sizes. The larger hooks are generally made of aluminum, lucite, plastic, or wood. The smaller hooks are usually steel. Most craft stores carry hooks, as do most yarn and "stitchery" stores. I prefer the Susan Bates hook for bead crochet, because you have to get the nose under the bead. The sharper nose makes it easier to go under the bead. Crochet hooks are very inexpensive, so you might want to try all of the brands available to see which one you like the best. Hook selection is a matter of personal preference.

The larger hooks are categorized by letter (B through N), while the steel hooks are sized by number. The earlier the letter in the alphabet, the smaller the hook. The lower the number, the bigger the hook. In addition to this slight confusion, the hook sizes may vary from company to company, even though they are labeled as the same size. For example, a Boye #9 hook may be 1.10 mm, while a Susan Bates #9 hook may be 1.25 mm. However, all hooks are marked with the dimension in millimeters, as well as the letter or number size. This will assist you in picking the hook that you want. When I suggest a hook size, I will describe it by both its number and its size in millimeters.

Which Hook for Which Yarn

Size #5 Yarn: Size C (3.25 mm) (You can decrease the size of your hook to 1.75 mm)
Size #10 Yarn: Size B (2.25 mm) (You can decrease the size of your hook to 1.6 mm)
Size #20 Yarn: Size 8 (1.4 mm) (You can decrease the size of your hook to 1.00 mm)
Size #30 Yarn: Size 9-10 (1.25 mm - 1.15 mm) (You can decrease the size of your hook to .90 mm)

Important Note: Should you use a hook that is much smaller than the smallest recommended size, it could:

1. Put a lot of pressure on the yarn, causing it to stiffen and stretch to such an extent as to lose both its drape and shape; and
2. Put excessive pressure on your arms and wrists (which, over a not-too-long time, could result in pain and potential injury).

Those things being said, the above chart is really just a "rule of thumb." Crocheting is the least "exact science" craft there is. Knitting needles tend to be uniform, as do beading needles. Not so in crochet. The end product is really your only test whether you are doing it properly. Hopefully, the above chart will give you some guidance, but, if there's a better combination for you, try it. I have found in my teaching that beginning bead crocheters tend to crochet very tightly, and, as they become at ease with the hook, they loosen up. Beaders who are new to crochet tend to be even tighter. As a result, you may find that you start with one size hook, but, after you've been bead crocheting for a while, you need to adjust your hook size. Further, I think you'll find that you use a smaller hook for slip-stitch bead crochet than you will for plain crochet.

Beads

Most of the seed beads available today are made in either Japan or the Czech Republic. The more popular of these two are the Japanese beads. They are more uniform (in size, color, and dye lot) than the Czech beads, and, therefore, are easier to use. The three major Japanese companies that are currently manufacturing seed beads (and exporting to the U.S.) are Miyuki, Toho, and Matsuno. Miyuki and Toho are usually interchangeable, but the Matsuno beads tend to run either a little larger or a little smaller, even though the label says they're the same. For example, many Matsuno #11's are larger than either Toho or Miyuki #11's. In fact, they seem to be about halfway between the #11's and #8's made by the other two companies. Matsuno #8's are also larger. The most popular sizes of seed beads used in crocheting run from #15's (1 mm), to #6's (4 mm). Both smaller (#22's) and larger (E beads, pony beads) are also manufactured, but, for the most part, you will be crocheting with beads in the more popular sizes. The Japanese companies also manufacture a small cylindrical bead. Miyuki calls them Delicas™, Toho calls them Treasures™ and Matsuno calls them Dynamites™. Cylinder beads are made in two sizes; 1.8 mm and 3.3 mm. The small cylinder beads are available in over 650 colors and finishes, but the large ones are available in a much more limited selection.

Bead finishes. While I won't claim to have listed all of the bead finishes potentially available, I will attempt to give you an overview.

Transparent. Clear bead, with color. Light can pass through this bead. Transparent beads are shiny.

Matte. A matte bead has an etched coating that changes the look of the surface from shiny to flat. Light does not easily pass through a matte bead. The word "matte" is often used interchangeably with the word "frosted," and sometimes "ghost."

Opaque. A solid color shiny bead, usually with very sharp (true) colors. No light can pass through this bead.

Luster. A high gloss coating which makes the color of the bead "gleam."

Gold Luster. Like luster, but having a goldish hue.

AB (aurora borealis), Iris (iridescent), or *Rainbow*. These beads have a coating that gives them a multi-color effect.

Silver-lined. These beads have an interior lining that is silver colored. This tends to enhance and sharpen the color of the bead, and often gives it a richer tone.

Gilt-lined (often used interchangeably with *Alabaster-lined*). These beads have an interior lining that is gold toned, which tends to soften the color and make it slightly warmer. It can create an opal effect as well.

Ceylon. These beads have a coating that gives a pearlized effect.

Galvanized. These beads have a metallic coating that is added after the bead is made, without a particularly good bonding adhesive, and hence may rub off. (There are ways to try to protect any beads against chipping, and these methods will be covered at the end of this chapter.)

Metallic. These beads have a very sharp finish that make the beads look like they are made of metal, although they rarely are. (Unlike galvanized, this finish rarely rubs off.)

Lined or color-lined. These beads either are two different colors or have an "inside" color with crystal on the outside. When they are color-lined, they tend to have the darker opaque color on the inside and the lighter transparent color on the outside, such as purple-lined pink, or orange-lined yellow.

Precious beads. These beads either have a plating of a precious (or semi-precious) metal, such as gold or copper, or are lined with metal (*e.g.*, copper-lined opal pink).

Bead shapes. Most beads are round, but not all. Any round bead will "bead crochet" easily, but there are other beads that are also fun to crochet. Try any bead with a hole at one end (such as a drop or a dagger), or any bead where all the sides are essentially the same (*e.g.*, any hex cut bead or Czech #9 three-cuts). The various shapes will give your pieces different looks, and some will even cause the piece to appear "flat."

How These Tools Interrelate

In very general terms:

1. The beads set the gauge.
2. The hook is always matched with the yarn.
3. The larger the beads, the heavier the yarn.

Now let's discuss some variations to these general rules and how they affect the results. Let's assume that you want more yarn to show (as a design factor). Either you could use a larger hook or you could use a heavier yarn than the bead calls for, or both. For example, let's assume that you want a very heavy, chunky rope, but you like a particular #8 seed bead. Instead of using #10 or #20 weight yarn, use #5 weight yarn. Then, depending on how much yarn you want to show, adjust your hook size: more yarn = larger hook; less yarn = smaller hook. In this example, the bead size alone will not set the gauge. Both the yarn and the hook size will also have an effect on it. The beads do control the gauge when they sit against each other tightly. For example, when you are using #30 weight yarn and #11 seed beads, the beads do indeed set the gauge. But, as you vary things, all three of your primary tools will affect the look and feel of your finished piece. Once you are at ease with basic bead crochet, try varying these things. When you do, your design options will expand enormously.

Miscellaneous Tools

The tools listed below will make your life as a bead crocheter easier.

Big "Eye" needle (sold at most bead stores). This needle is the easiest way I know to string or "load" the beads.

Collapsible eye needle (sold at most bead stores). If the hole in the bead is too small to accommodate the Big "Eye" needle and yarn, try using this needle.

Jewelers cement (sold at bead stores, craft stores, and some jewelry stores). If you are a security nut (and many of us are), glue your knots with this.

Nail polish top coat. If none of the needles listed above works, brush the end of the yarn with a thin coat of top coat making a "self-needle" at the end.

This may end your "loading" crisis. (If this doesn't work, you may be stuck crocheting with either #50 weight or #80 weight yarn.)

Kacha-Kacha (sold at many bead stores, and at knitting stores). A counting tool. It can keep track of either the number of stitches or rounds, or both. It's useful in stringing patterns as well as for counting rounds.

Skirt (or kilt) pin (sold in most craft and fabric stores). This is handy as a stitch holder. It has a very firm closure, so it will not open by itself (thereby allowing all your hard work to pull out in an instant). It's also handy when you need to pull out some stitches and need to "catch" the loop of the last stitch you want pulled out. It's much sturdier than a safety pin, and it's less likely to pierce the thread.

Tapestry needle (sold in most craft, fabric, and knitting stores). Try to find a thin one. You will often need it to weave things together.

#10 Beading needle (sold in most bead stores). Helpful in fixing mistakes, grafting pieces together, as well as for making fringe.

#12 Beading needle (sold in most bead stores). Not as sturdy as #10, but necessary at times.

Lollypop or T pins (sold in some knitting stores, and almost all fabric stores). Used for blocking.

Long nose tweezers (OPTIONAL). Some people prefer to grab a loop with a pair of tweezers rather than a pin so that they absolutely don't risk splitting the yarn.

Small sharp pointy scissors. You want to be able to get the point of the scissor where you want it.

Chain nose pliers (available at most bead stores, some craft stores, and some hardware stores). Important for breaking a bead. Also needed if you plan to use wire in the finishing work.

Round nose pliers (available at most bead stores, some craft stores, and some hardware stores). Needed for finishing work done with wire.

Wire cutter (available at most bead stores, some craft stores, and some hardware stores). Needed for finishing work done with wire.

Findings, etc. (available at most bead stores). Includes bead caps, cones, eyepins, clasps, 20 and 22 gauge wire in silver and gold-filled. Used primarily in finishing work.

Sleeves (OPTIONAL) (sold in most places that sell the crochet hooks, craft stores, some bead stores, and most "stitchery" and knitting stores). These are rubber "sleeves" for crochet hooks that might help if arthritis is a problem for you. With a drop of either soap or oil, they slide on and off the hooks easily. The other good news is that they are very inexpensive (between $2.00 and $3.00), so you can afford to try one and throw it away if you don't like it.

Wrist and/or arm supports (OPTIONAL) (sold in most drugstores and even some grocery stores). If you become addicted to bead crochet (and I'm sure that you will) and find that you are doing it often, it would be wise to protect against potential injuries or strain. Most of the twisting in bead crochet is in the wrist, therefore a wrist stabilizer can help. If you don't like it or find it uncomfortable, there are some lightweight elasticized arm/elbow supports that also help protect against injury.

Krylon® (available at most hardware and craft stores). Used for protecting or sealing the coating of beads to avoid tarnishing or chipping. Place the beads that you wish to protect in a plastic bag. Hold the nozzle inside the bag, and clutch the bag around the spray nozzle on the can of Krylon®. Spray the Krylon® into the bag for thirty to sixty seconds. Remove the can and give the bag a good shake. Pour the beads into a small plastic tub with a secure top. Let them dry for a few minutes, then put the top on the plastic tub and give it a good shake. Repeat the entire process once or twice more, and allow the beads to dry.

Polyurethane spray. Also used to protect and seal beads that have a finish that can chip off or tarnish. It should outlast and outperform the Krylon®, but is more difficult to apply. Place the beads in a paper bag, and spray the polyurethane into the bag. Keep shaking the beads to make sure that all are well coated. Then place in a shallow aluminum baking tray that comes with a plastic lid. Punch air holes in the lid and then place it on the pan. Every ten to fifteen minutes, give the pan a good shake to insure that the beads don't stick to the bottom or each other. The drying time can be as long as four hours.

Tips of the Trade
Bead Crochet

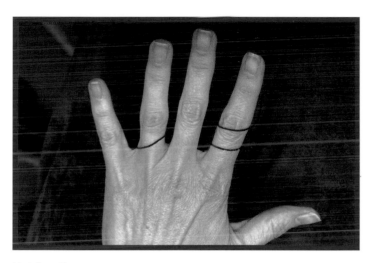

Holding the yarn.

be wobbly when you work. Then place your thumb on the flat part of the hook. The combination of the index finger and thumb positioned correctly is what gives you control over the movement of the hook. (Without maximum control, your work will never be even, and it will go more slowly than is fun!)

Holding the yarn. (Note: You can reverse this as shown in the picture above.) Holding the yarn properly is very important. It helps you maintain tension, increases your speed, and protects your wrist (as much as possible, given the "twisting" motion of crochet). The working yarn is held by your non-dominant hand. Lay the yarn over the pinky, under the ring finger, over the middle finger, then over and around the index finger. This is not as complicated as it sounds, and it becomes automatic when you have been crocheting for a while.

Holding the hook.

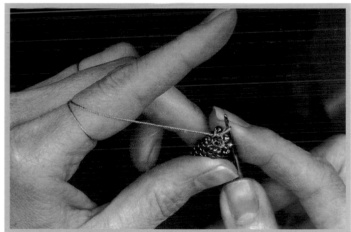

Holding the work.

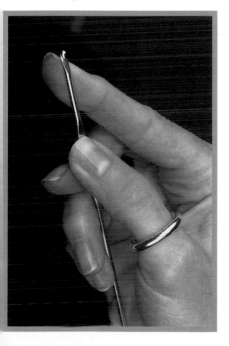

Holding the hook. With the "nose" of the hook facing you, place your index finger (on your dominant hand) on the side of the hook that is away from your body, about 1/8 to 1/4 inch from the top of the hook. Positioning your finger this way will allow you to control the hook. If your index finger is too far from the top of the hook, your hook will

Holding the work. Once you have your work started (directions are in "Bead chaining" below), hold the work in between the thumb of your non-dominant hand on one side of the yarn (or work) and your middle finger on the other side of the work. As you are working, hold the worked piece down (towards the floor) with these two fingers. The combination of this holding position and the way you hold the yarn, as described above, is what enables you to control the tension. (Note: Most people tend to maintain a very tight tension when they begin bead crochet. As they relax, they loosen it. If this is the case for you, change to a hook that is one size larger than the one that is called for until you feel more at ease and your tension loosens. There will be more tips on tension throughout this chapter.)

Slip-stitch bead crochet.

Bead chaining. Make the usual slip knot to begin your work. Bring up a bead, using either the index or middle finger of your dominant hand. Holding the bead against the hook, make a chain stitch. The bead will sit right in the middle of the chain. If your tension is too loose, the bead will slip through the stitch. If your tension is too tight, you'll find out in the next round because you won't be able to get your hook under the bead.

Joining. Hold the five to nine beads you have chained in a circle with the beads facing outward. The first and last beads chained should be sitting right next to each other. With the nose of the hook facing downward, stick the tip of your hook under the first bead you chained. (Your hook will be pointing toward the left and at a slight upward tilt when you do this.) The bead will be touching the hook. Flip the bead you've just gone under to the right side of the hook. Pull up the next bead on the yarn, making sure that it's sitting on top of the bead from the round before. Turn the nose of the hook upward (to the right), and grab the working yarn with the hook and pull it through both loops of yarn currently on your hook. (You can either pull the yarn through both loops at once or, if you find that difficult, pull it through one loop at a time.) You have just joined your bead chains into a tube using the slip-stitch method of bead crochet. (Note: It is very important that your working yarn is held up and to the left, and it must be OVER (on top of) both beads when you slip-stitch. If not, the yarn will get caught on the bead of the previous round and pull that bead into the center of your tube. (You will understand this better once you have begun to work. It happens to everyone, but less and less as you gain experience.)

These instructions are for right-handed people. If you are left-handed, sit in front of a mirror, and the mirror image should be as described above.

Slip-stitch crochet. To continue, stick the nose of the hook under the next bead, flip the bead to the right, pull up the next bead string on the yarn, adjust

the hook, and then pull the yarn through the two loops that are on the hook just as you did above. Keep going, making sure that you are always going under the immediate next bead. If you skip a bead, or pick up one from the row below, you will not have an even tube.

Increasing. There may be times that, for design reasons, you want to know how to increase the size of your tube. It's really quite easy. Insert the hook under the bead, as always. Pull up a bead, and pull the yarn through. Now put the hook back under the SAME bead again. Pull up another bead and pull the yarn through. The beads will appear a little crowded in that first round, but will even out and look correct after the following round.

Decreasing. You'll find many uses for this technique. There are two ways to decrease.

1. Make a beadless slip-stitch in the stitch where you want to decrease. In the next round, skip that stitch entirely.

2. Insert the hook under the bead. Do not pull up a bead. Pull the yarn through the stitch but not through the loop on your hook, leaving two loops of yarn on your hook. Go under the next bead, pull up a bead, then pull the yarn through all three loops on your hook.

Although the first method seems to be more popular, I prefer the second method. It's a neater way to decrease in that it is virtually invisible.

Changing yarn. To change yarn, cut the old working thread, leaving a 4 to 6-inch tail. Using the tail, make an extra beadless chain, and pull the tail through that chain. Now go under the bead that you added last. Double the new working yarn, making a loop. (The short end of the new yarn does not need to be more than two to three inches.) Pull the loop under the last crocheted bead. Grab both sides of the new working yarn and make a beadless chain stitch with both sides of the yarn. Pull the loop until the short end comes free. (You will now have two loose ends sitting in the middle of your tube.) Slip-stitch crochet several rounds, with the two loose ends in the center of the tube, to make sure that you like the connection, that the pattern matches, etc. When you are sure that all is sitting right, knot the two tails together in the center of the tube, being careful to pull both ends tight while creating the knot. Cut the tails 1/4 to 3/4 inch from the knot, and continue to crochet as before. (Note: If you cut the yarn too close to the knot, it can come undone easily.) If you like, you can also glue the knot with jewelers cement.

Bead single crochet. Although most of this book uses the slip-stitch method of bead crochet, I want to tell you how to do a bead single crochet. Again, there are two ways.

1. Bring up a bead, then do a single crochet locking it into place.

2. Start your single crochet. When you have two loops on your hook, bring up a bead, then finish the stitch, locking the bead into the center of the stitch.

Either of these methods works fine. I think that the second method is a bit better in that the beads tend to sit much more evenly.

The Most Common Mistakes Made in Slip-Stitch Bead Crochet

A recessed bead. When you see a recessed bead (one that sits more toward the center of the tube than it should), you probably caught the working yarn under the bead in the previous row. Pull out the last few stitches until you get back to the recessed bead. Hold your yarn, in an exaggerated manner, up and to the left. Using the middle finger on your dominant hand, hold the bead from the previous row down, and then make your stitch. If you notice a recessed bead way back in your tube and are unwilling to pull out your work, there are several ways to try to fix it. Insert a size #1 knitting needle into the tube and see if it forces the recessed bead out. If not, stick a #10 beading needle through the hole of the recessed bead until the bead is in the center of the needle. Gently pull both ends of the needle until the bead pops up over the yarn that is holding it down.

A protruding bead. Usually when you have a protruding bead, it's because you forgot to flip the bead over the hook to the right before stitching. The easy way to fix this is to pull out the stitches until you get back to the protruding bead. If you notice a protruding bead way back in your tube and are unwilling to go back, there's another way to fix it. Thread a #10 beading needle with Silamide. Anchor the thread a few rows back on the same diagonal line of beads as the protruding bead. (To anchor the thread, make a knot, and catch the thread in a stitch so that you are unable to see the knot, but so that it holds securely.) Run the needle and thread through the line of beads ending with the protruding bead. Then anchor the needle and thread in the tube. If you anchor the thread immediately after you pass the needle through the protruding bead, it will force the bead to lie flat against the tube.

A shrinking tube. As you are working, you may notice that your tube has become thinner. If this happens, you skipped a stitch or two. There's no way to fix this other than to pull out your work until you get back to a row with the same number of beads as were in the original tube.

You can't see where you're going. Put the "loop" that is currently on your hook onto a skirt pin. Then stick the butt end of the hook down your crocheted tube. The beads that are to be worked next should snuggle against the hook. You should be able to count the same number of beads around as you used to begin your tube. If not, pull out the work until you can do this.

If this is your first project and you are having trouble seeing where to go, try this: Using Opera #5, string your beads alternating six matte beads with six shiny beads. Chain the first six matte beads, and then form them into a tube using a shiny bead. Each time you go under a matte bead, you should be bringing up a shiny one. Similarly, when you go under a shiny bead, you should be bringing up a matte one. At all times, you should be able to count six beads around, and the butt end of the hook should not bump into a bead if you stick it down into the tube.

A lumpy tube. You probably went underneath the bead of the previous row. Again, the only way to fix this is to pull out your work until you undo the "lump."

"Wobbly" beads. Your tension is too loose or uneven. If your tension is too loose, try going down (smaller) one hook size. If the problem persists, try this: Take out an extra ball of yarn in the same size as you are using and just chain without any beads. Continue practicing this until it becomes mindless and your stitches are even. (Even if you're a veteran crocheter, it's a good idea to do a short chaining exercise when you are changing the yarn and hook by several sizes.)

You can't get the nose of your hook under the bead. Your tension is too tight. Go up (larger) a hook size (or two, if necessary). If this doesn't work, try the simple chaining exercise described above. (No one likes the chaining exercises, and everyone benefits from them.)

Too-twisted tube. You've been working for a while, and all of a sudden your tube doesn't seem to want to turn. This happens more often as your piece gets longer. Stand up. Run your thumb and index finger from the ball of yarn down towards the work, and then just hold it. It will untwist itself.

Time to rest. Your beads are all strung and you want to put your work away until later and not worry about whether you'll come back to find it in a knot. You can either (1) wrap the loaded yarns around the ball and then put a piece of scotch tape loosely over the wrapped yarn or (2) get a bobbin at a knitting store and wrap the loaded yarn onto it. I actually prefer the first way. It is faster and easier and requires only scotch tape.

Bead Stringing or Loading

How much should I string? When stringing beads, it's wise not to string much more than 3 to 6 feet at a time for the following reasons:

1. If you make a stringing mistake, you might have to remove all the beads. In this situation, better less than more.

2. No matter how durable your yarn, running 10 yards of beads up and down it as you crochet could wear the yarn, and potentially cause it to "fuzz" a bit, or even fray (particularly if the edges of the beads are not smooth).

Simple stringing. Put the yarn through the middle of a Big "Eye" needle, and load the beads. In a simple repeated pattern, leave one sequence of the pattern on the yarn when you are changing yarn. That way, when you string more beads, you can copy what you've already done.

Complicated patterns. For a complicated pattern, there are lots of tricks. One of them will probably work for you.

1. Enlarge the pattern on a copying machine. Place a Post-it® under the line (row) of the pattern that you are working on. Move the Post-it® to the next row immediately after finishing each row. At the same time, as a failsafe, click the Kacha-Kacha. It will also keep track of your rows for you.

2. Write the pattern for each row on a separate index card, and flip the card when you finish the row. You can always add a Kacha-Kacha to this method, too, if you feel the need for a safeguard.

3. Segregate one entire sequence of beads by putting scotch tape at each end. After loading the next sequence, compare the two to make sure they are identical.

When you are starting a complicated pattern that doesn't show itself for a while, it is easier to avoid making a mistake by doing the following: If you are crocheting 6 around, bring up 6 beads at a time. Likewise, if you are crocheting 8 around, bring up 8 beads at a time for the first several rounds. Once you see the pattern emerge, you can revert to bringing up as many beads as you can handle comfortably.

Stringing mistakes.

1. An extra bead. This one is easy to fix. Break the extra bead using chain nose pliers. Make sure you cover the bead with one hand so that when the glass shatters, it doesn't fly up and cut you.

2. Missing a bead. There are two ways to handle this.

a. Make a beadless slip-stitch, and later on, go back and sew in a bead, making sure that the added bead is sewn on the same angle as the rest of the beads.

b. End the yarn. Thread the missing bead on the yarn, and continue as you would when you change yarn.

The second method is preferable. It really doesn't require a lot of extra time, and it's fairly difficult to align the "sewn-in" bead so that it looks like it has been crocheted

Sculptural Slip-Stitch Bead Crochet

This is a fancy way to say changing the size or shape of the beads within the piece to get a sculptural or dimensional effect. A simple example of this would be to make raised relief flowers within the piece. To do this, first graph the flowers using a bead crochet graph that reflects how many beads around you will be using. If you are working primarily with #11 seed beads, make your raised relief flowers with #8 seed beads.

You can change bead sizes and shapes at will. It does not have to have an even step-by-step progression from the smallest bead to the largest bead, although it can be. An elongated sculptural spiral could be accomplished by starting with #15's and going up to #6's in the same row. For example, your stringing sequence could be two #15's, three #11's, one #9 three-cut, one #8, one #6, and one #9 three-cut (crocheted 9 around). This is probably an exaggeration of what you would do, however, string on several sequences just to see how this crochet looks. You can also make the piece look flat by adding drops or daggers across from each other on both sides of the tube. The variations of the kinds of "sculpting" you can create are virtually limitless. Some of the mistakes addressed above are even more likely to happen, so be a bit more careful when sculpting. It is very easy to miss (skip) a stitch when there is a #15 or a small cylinder squeezed between two #8 seed beads. It's also easier to catch your yarn under a bead if it happens to be larger than the one you are adding. Sculptural work is slower work than when all the beads are the same size, but I think that you'll find the results to be worth it.

Blocking

Blocking is a way of "stabilizing" the yarn so it will neither grow nor shrink, but rather hold the length and shape that you have given it. In bead crochet, as in all crochet, your work might grow unless you either vary one of the tools or block your work. If you prefer not to change any of your tools, you'll find it very easy to block the material. Since blocking requires drying time, you may wish to do it when you are sure you are finished working for the day. Both cotton and silk will dry easily overnight.

For cotton, pin one end to a terry cloth towel with a lollipop (or T) pin. Pull the tube to get the excess "stretch" out, and then pin the other end to the towel as well. (Don't over-pull it unless you want it to stay that way.) Take a look (and feel) to make sure that you like what you have done, and then spray it with cold water. The piece will retain the new length if you have done as described above.

In the case of silk, just wet the piece under cold tap water, and lay it on the towel. Pull to the length that you'd like it. (There's no need to pin, and, in fact, pinning silk might damage the material.) When it dries, it will also retain this length. Again, take out the excess stretch, but don't over-stretch it.

Swatching

Whenever you aren't sure how a piece will look, string a foot or two of beads and make a "swatch" (small piece), so that you can look at it carefully. Make sure you like it before starting a 45-inch lariat, only to decide halfway through you don't like the way the colors look together. Most people don't like to swatch, but, from experience, I can tell you it saves time and aggravation in the long run. (If you can't stand to work on anything that doesn't turn into something, turn your swatches into earrings.)

Bead Crochet: The Structure of Your Pieces

Technically, when you bead crochet, regardless of whether you are slip-stitching or using the single crochet method, you are stitching the beads into the WRONG side of the work. To see how this happens,

make a small square (using either crochet method), and crochet a bead into every other stitch as you work back and forth. You'll notice that one row of beads is on one side of the piece, and the next row is on the other. In both cases, you'll see that the beads are on the side of the work that is facing away from you. To compensate for this peculiarity, most bead crocheted pieces are done in the round (tubular), and you are actually wearing them inside-out.

As a result of the above, and because you are using yarn with the beads (rather than Silamide thread or Nymo®), turning your work into structured pieces requires just a little bit of new thought. I will attempt to give you structural ideas for your pieces to get you started. But, as in all beadwork, should you come up with another way that works and looks good...use it.

Finishing techniques.

1. *No clasp*. To attach a bracelet or necklace to itself with no clasp, try either one of the following:

a. It's important to complete an entire sequence prior to joining the two ends, or your pattern won't match. Thread a #10 beading needle with Silamide that matches your work. Anchor your thread 3 or 4 rows from the end of the tube. Hold the two ends of the tube together with the pattern matching. Run the needle and thread up through the column of beads on one end of the tube. Then run the needle and thread through the matching column on the other end of the tube. Anchor the thread after you have gone through 3 to 4 rows of beads on this end of the tube. Move over one row of beads. Insert the needle and thread, and run it through three or four rows of beads and then back into the end of the tube where you started. Go up three to five rows, re-anchor the thread, move over one column of beads, and repeat. Continue around the tube until you are convinced that the two ends of the tube are securely attached to each other. Vary the number of rows on either end of the tube to avoid getting a "hem-line" look, *i.e.*, go up three to four beads on one end, and when you return to this same end, go up either two or six beads before anchoring the thread.

b. Do as above, but connect only one row of beads on each end of the tube. This will act like a "basting." Now thread a thin tapestry needle with a foot or two of yarn and anchor it in the tube. Go under a bead of the last row you crocheted. Flip the bead as you would when crocheting it. Now come across to the other end of the tube and, working on a slight zigzag, catch the small piece of yarn holding the matching stitch on the other end. Pull the needle and thread through, from the inside of the tube to the outside of the tube. Going back to the first end, catch the next stitch under the bead and then flip the bead. Continue working back and forth around the tube. Be very careful not to skip a bead in your original chain. If done correctly, the joining of the two ends of the tube will not show. If the connection feels at all loose to you, repeat around the tube. There is no need to flip the bead when you go around the tube a second time.

The first method is the easier way, but many people like the strength of the second method. The second method will take a bit of practice. You can also combine the two methods by doing the first in its entirety, and then connecting one or two stitches with the yarn.

2. *Finishing with a clasp*. There are several ways to attach a clasp to your work, and each will give you a slightly different "look."

a. Use a 2 to 4-inch eyepin (or a piece of 20 or 22 gauge wire on which you have made a very small loop at the end). When you look at the eyepin, you will notice that the wire of the loop does not quite touch of the wire of the stem. Take chain nose pliers and squeeze the loop so that the wire does touch the wire of the stem. Then thread the tail of your working yarn onto a thin tapestry needle. Sink the eyepin (or wire) into the end of the tube and sew through the closed loop of the eyepin (or the loop you made with the wire). Anchor the yarn, and pass the needle back through the eyepin. Repeat until the loop of the eyepin is filled with yarn. Don't worry about how this looks, as it will never be seen. Cut the yarn close to the work. Thread a bead cap or cone over the stem of the eyepin, making sure that you cover the attachment. Attach the eyepin to a clasp with a wrapped loop.

b. Thread a tapestry needle with the tail of your yarn. Thread the needle through a bead cap or cone, and then through the hole of a clamshell bead tip. At this point you could simply make a knot that is big enough that it doesn't slip back through the hole in the clamshell. If you prefer, you can run the thread through a bead that is small enough to fit inside a clamshell and then return the needle and thread back through the hole in the clamshell, through the cone, and into the bead crocheted tube. Then, anchor the thread in the tube.

c. Using a plug bead to end your tube. Find a bead that fits nicely into your tube, but doesn't disappear inside. Thread a #10 beading needle with matching Silamide and sew the plug bead into the tube. Go through the bead and tube several times, but leave enough space so that a piece of 20 to 22 gauge wire can also fit through the hole in the bead. Insert a 3-inch piece of wire through the plug bead. Bend the wire that is exiting each side of the plug bead so that it forms an X over the plug bead. Where

the wire crosses itself, bend each side "up" (away from the bead). The two sides of the wire will be parallel to each other and perpendicular to the bead. Clip one side of the wire so that it is about 1/4 inch long. Start making a wrapped loop with the longer side of the wire by making a ninety degree angle where the short piece of the wire ends. Thread one side of the clasp on the wire. Finish making your wrapped loop, making sure that you wrap this wire around both the short and the long ends of the wire.

3. *Attaching your tube to a lampwork bead*. Like everything else, there's more than one way to affix a large bead to your work. It can be done with or without a clasp. If you are doing it with a clasp, you will need two pieces of crocheted tubes. They can be equal lengths or not, as you choose.

a. Attaching the lampwork (or large) bead with yarn only. First take a good look at the bead. Is the side of the bead flat around the hole, or does the bead recess inward where the hole is? Knowing this enables you to finish your tube in a way that will make the attachment neater. If the bead is broad and flat, do a row of beadless chains. If the hole recesses, you will want to taper the tube by decreasing the number of stitches. For the first round of decreases, working with beads, decrease two to three stitches evenly around the tube. Then, without beads, slip-stitch and decrease another two to three stitches around the tube. (You may find that you need to decrease only in the last beadless chain round.) The amount you decrease will depend upon the lampwork bead you are using. Thread two thin tapestry needles with the yarn from each end (side) of the tube. Going in opposite directions, pass the needles through the center of your large bead. Then, working with one side at a time, catch a piece of the yarn that is right under a bead and pull the needle so that your working yarn is very tight, snugging the bead up against the tube. Then cross the tube on the perpendicular and catch the yarn of the stitch directly across the tube on the other side. Then pass the needle and yarn back through the center of the large bead. Using the other needle, do the same thing on the other side, then pass the needle back through the bead. Move ninety degrees to the right on each side of the tube and repeat what you just did. This will ensure that the bead is securely fastened to both sides of the tube. Repeat as many times as you feel necessary to give your focal bead sufficient support. You may wish to anchor the yarn further up in the tube if you are working with a heavier bead. In that case, anchor both ends of yarn in the tube.

b. Using wire to support your focal bead. Make a wrapped loop on one end of a 3-inch piece of wire, or use an eyepin. Attach the eyepin as in "Finishing with a clasp" above. Then begin making a wrapped loop at the other end of the wire that you've just attached. Thread a soldered jump ring into the loop, and wrap it. Insert a piece of 18 or 20 gauge wire through the lampwork or focal bead, with 2 to 3 inches of wire extending from each side of the bead. On each side of the bead, make a wrapped loop and attach it to the soldered jump ring that is joined to the end of the tube. If you would like your focal bead to have "movement," leave extra wire on each side of it. If you would like it to be stationary, wrap the wire so that it holds the bead in place. It will probably take more than one "wrap."

4. *Adding beads and fringe to the bottom of a lariat.*

a. If you want to add a lampwork bead to the bottom of a lariat without any fringe, you will need at least one pivot bead that is large enough that it doesn't get "swallowed" by the lampwork bead. In this case, thread the tail of the yarn from which you made the piece onto the smallest needle that fits. Exiting the tube, run the needle through the lampwork bead, through the pivot bead and back up the lampwork bead. Anchor the thread inside the tube. Repeat until the lampwork bead is secure.

b. Adding a lampwork bead and fringe: Thread your yarn onto the smallest needle possible. (If you are using #30 weight yarn, it will thread onto a #10 beading needle. Not so if you are using thicker yarn.) Thread another beading needle with several yards of Silamide in a color that matches your work. Pull the ends of the thread even to double it if you are making "looped" fringe, and leave it single if you are making straight fringe. Knot the end, and anchor the thread inside the tube. Bring both needles through the lampwork bead and make a fringe with each. Making one strand of the fringe with the working yarn will give extra stability to your work. If the hole in your lampwork bead is sufficiently large that your "fringe beads" ride up into it, try stuffing the bead with a pipe cleaner (or two), leaving just enough room for your needle and thread to pass through the bead. (The pipe cleaner can be removed easily once there is enough fringe to prevent "creeping.") Re-anchor both the yarn and the thread inside the tube, and continue making the additional fringe you want with the Silamide. (Refer to 3a above to see if you want to decrease the end of the tube prior to attaching the bead and fringe.)

Increasing and decreasing evenly. Should you wish to increase or decrease within the tube, and want to do so by more than one stitch, divide the increases (decreases) evenly around the tube. If you increase all in one place you will get a ruffled effect. If you decrease all in one place, you will cause one place in the tube to have an indentation.

Torque. As you crochet your tube, you'll notice that the beads twist around to your left, creating a torqued effect. Actually, with each round, you are moving a half stitch to the left. If the piece does not torque, you are doing something wrong. When you are designing a pattern, it is important to remember that the stitches move by a half stitch.

Maintaining a tube. At some point, as you increase the number of stitches in your tube, the tube will flatten out. Unfortunately, I cannot give you the exact number of stitches that will cause this. It depends upon your hook size relative to the yarn size, as well as what type of yarn you are using. It's also affected by whether you are "sculpting" your work. However, in broad generalities, it is safe to assume that you will maintain a tube crocheting 9 beads around. It is also safe to say that your tube will flatten if you crochet 18 beads around. If you use a very small hook relative to the yarn, you can crochet more stitches around before your tube flattens. If you use a large hook relative to the yarn, your tube will flatten sooner. (You may, in fact, want a flattened tube. For example, maybe you are making a wide cuff and would like the piece to sit flat.) Likewise, if you use silk, your tube will flatten sooner than if you use cotton. If you are unsure whether your tube will flatten, make a swatch that is at least 4 inches long. At that length, you should be able to tell.

Blocking. Because you are using yarn, there's always a chance your piece can "grow." (Using bonded nylon or polyester thread will not necessarily prevent this.) If you want to be sure just how long your piece will be and do not want it to grow, be sure to block the piece when it is several inches shorter than the final length you want. (Follow the "blocking" instructions in the first part of this chapter.) Be sure to do this early enough in your work, as you may be surprised at how long the piece really is after it has been mildly stretched. Leave the working yarn attached during the blocking. Should your blocked piece end up longer than you would like, pull your work out until you reach the desired length.

Bead Crochet Projects
Introduction to Bead Crochet Projects

The following projects are in order from the easiest to the most difficult, much like a tutorial. Each new project will introduce either a new technique(s), a new tool(s), or both. If you skip one or more of the projects and find that you get "stuck," go back to an earlier project to see if your problem is solved. I do not repeat the very basic instructions more than once or twice. For example, in the early projects, I tell you how to put the yarn through a Big "Eye" needle to load or string the beads. In the later projects, I say only "load" or "string" the beads. If you find yourself unsure of how to do this, simply refer back to an earlier project.

A few small points prior to beginning. In an effort to accommodate size changes, I have deliberately listed larger quantities of the beads than you'll need for each project. At the end of every project, I have listed the exact supplies (including the bead manufacturer and color number) that I used in that particular project. If you have any difficulty finding any of these products, see the "Resources" section in the back of this book and you'll find one or more sources for each item.

In every case, when #30 weight crochet cotton is recommended, you can substitute either #20 weight crochet cotton or size #8 Perle cotton.

If you find that you like both the projects and their progression, and hence do each and every one in order, by the time you finish, you will definitely be a master of bead crochet.

Enjoy your bead crochet journey.

Project 1
Basic 24-Inch Bead Crochet Necklace

This project is made using a "fat" yarn and large beads. I suggest that you try this project first so that mistakes can be seen easily, and, hopefully, corrected. For example, if your tube looks lumpy when you have done several rounds, pull the yarn out very slowly. At the same time, look carefully at the tube. The yarn should never be UNDER the bead as you pull the yarn out. If it is, you probably caught the yarn under the bead when you flipped the bead over to the right. Make sure that the yarn is OVER (on top of) the beads prior to slip stitching. If the yarn is under the bead, it will pull the bead towards the center of the tube, making it almost impossible to see which beads should be crocheted next.

Materials and Tools Needed

110 grams #6 seed beads
#5 weight crochet cotton or Perle cotton #3
Size B (2.25 mm) crochet hook
Big "Eye" needle
Tapestry needle
**Two 3-inch eyepins or 6 inches of 20 or 22
 gauge wire**
Two bead caps or cones
Clasp
Chain nose pliers
Round nose pliers
Wire cutter
Scissors

Proceed as follows:

Thread 3 inches of yarn through the center of the Big "Eye" needle. Using that needle, load 3 to 5 feet of beads onto the yarn. Bead chain 6 beads. Join into a tube using a bead slip-stitch. Crochet the entire tube 6 around. It will be necessary to change thread in this project. (Refer back to the "Tips" chapter of this book if you need a refresher on how to do this.) When the piece is approximately 20 inches, block it to see how long it really is, and to "set" it. Continue slip-stitch crocheting until the piece measures 23 inches. Do one additional round of beadless slip stitches, decreasing 2 stitches in that round.

Cut the 6-inch piece of wire in half. Make a small loop (wrapped once) at one end of each piece of wire. Using the tail of the yarn and the tapestry needle, sew one of the wire loops to one end of the tube. Repeat with the second piece of wire at the other end of the tube. Feed a bead cap or a cone over each piece of wire. Attach the wires to a clasp with a wrapped loop.

For this project, I used:
1. Miyuki seed beads in color #454
2. Opera #5 crochet cotton in color #562
3. Bali bead caps
4. Vermeil clasp

Basic 24-Inch Bead Crochet Necklace

Project 2
Chunky 24-Inch Necklace

This project is made with thinner yarn than the first project. The necklace also contains an easy spiral pattern, which will require you to pay more attention when you are loading (stringing) the beads. You will notice with this pattern that you are pulling up a bead that is the same color and finish as the bead your hook has just gone under. If not, either you made a stringing mistake, or you skipped a stitch (thereby shrinking the tube). If you find an error, try to figure out how you made it, which will help you avoid repeating it in the future when the stringing sequences become more complicated.

Materials and Tools Needed

30 grams main color (MC) #8 seed beads (A)
20 grams contrasting color 1 (CC1) #8 seed beads (B)
20 grams contrasting color 2 (CC2) #8 seed beads (C)
#10 weight crochet cotton
Size #4 (1.75 mm) crochet hook
Big "Eye" needle
Tapestry needle
Two bead caps (or cones)
Two 3-inch eyepins or 6 inches of 20 to 22 gauge wire, cut in half
Clasp
Chain nose pliers
Round nose pliers
Wire cutter
Scissors

Proceed as follows:

Pull a 3-inch piece of yarn through the center of the Big "Eye" needle. Using the Big "Eye" needle to pick up the beads, string on the following sequence of beads: Four MC beads, one CC1 bead, two CC2 beads, one CC1 bead. This sequence will be used throughout the project.

Bead chain 8 stitches (one complete sequence). Join with a bead slip-stitch, and crochet 8 around. The three different color beads will make a spiral pattern in your necklace because the crochet stitches move a half stitch to the left each and every round. Continue to slip-stitch crochet until your necklace is 23 inches long. For the final round, do one round of slip stitches without using beads, and at the same time, decrease 3 stitches in this last round. Block the tube.

Close the loop of the eyepin by squeezing the loop with chain nose pliers. (Instead of using an eyepin, you can substitute a piece of 20 or 22 gauge wire on which you've made a small loop at one end.) Using the yarn and a tapestry needle, sew the eyepin into the center of one end of the tube. Do the same on the other end of the tube with the other eyepin. Thread a bead cap or cone onto each eyepin. Holding the bead cap firmly against the tube, join the eyepins to a clasp using a wrapped loop.

For this project, I used:
1. Toho #8 seed beads in color #166DF
2. Miyuki #8 seed beads in color #459
3. Toho #8 seed beads in color #928
4. Cébélia® #10 crochet cotton in color #3052
5. Silver clasp from India
6. Hill Tribe silver tulip bead caps

WE HOPE THAT YOU ENJOY THIS BOOK...and that it will occupy a proud place in your library. We would like to keep you informed about other publications from Schiffer Books. Please return this card with your requests and comments. **(Please print clearly in ink.)**
Note: We don't share our mailing list with anyone.

Title of Book Purchased _____
❑ Purchased at: _____ ❑ received as a gift
Comments or ideas for books you would like to see us publish: _____

_____

Your Name: _____
Address _____
City _____ State_____ Zip_____ Country_____

E-mail Address _____
Please provide your email address to receive announcements of new releases

❑ Please send me a **free** *Schiffer Antiques, Collectibles, & the Arts*
❑ Please send me a **free** *Schiffer Woodcarving, Woodworking, and Crafts Catalog*
❑ Please send me a **free** *Schiffer Military, Aviation, and Automotive History Catalog*
❑ Please send me a **free** *Schiffer Lifestyle, Design, and Body, Mind, & Spirit Catalog*

See our most current books on the web at **www.schifferbooks.com**
Contact us at: Phone: 610-593-1777; Fax: 610-593-2002; or E-mail: info@schifferbooks.com
SCHIFFER BOOKS ARE CURRENTLY AVAILABLE FROM YOUR BOOKSELLER

K: user\do\wp\basic\bouceback

Printed in China

For the latest releases and
thousands of books in print,
fill out the back of this card
and return it today!

SCHIFFER PUBLISHING LTD
4880 LOWER VALLEY ROAD
ATGLEN, PA 19310-9717 USA

I...III.I....II....IIII...I.I..I...I...III...II...II...II...II.I.I

Chunky 24-Inch Necklace

Project 3
45-Inch Lariat Made
with #9 Three-Cut Beads

In this project, you will reduce the yarn size yet another time. You'll also attach lampwork beads with fringe.

Materials and Tools Needed

2-1/2 hanks of #9 three-cut Czech beads
Size 8 (1.4 mm) crochet hook
#20 weight crochet cotton
Big "Eye" needle
Collapsible eye needle
#10 beading needles
Silamide to match
Crystals for the fringe
Two end (focal) beads
Scissors
One pipe cleaner

Proceed as follows:
Load 3 to 5 feet of beads onto the yarn as described in Projects 1 and 2. Crochet 6 around until the lariat measures approximately 36 inches. Block the lariat to see how long it really is and to "set" it. Remember that heavier beads are going on the ends, so make sure you get out all the excess stretch, or the lampwork beads will cause the piece to grow while you are wearing it. When your lariat is 42 inches (or the desired length), do one final row of beadless slip stitches, decreasing 3 stitches in that last round.

Using two #10 beading needles, thread one needle with 1/2 yard of matching #30 weight cotton and the other with 3 yards of matching Silamide, doubled. Anchor both needles into one end of the tube. Thread both needles through a lampwork bead (or any other focal or end bead), then plug the bead with the pipe cleaner. Make one looped fringe with each needle, using a heavier crystal at the bottom of the fringe. Pass the needles back through your focal bead and anchor the thread and yarn in the tube. Make the remaining fringe using the Silamide. Secure the thread several inches up into the tube. Repeat on the other end of the tube.

For this project, I used:
1. #9 three-cut Czech beads in Garnet AB
2. Flora #20 weight crochet cotton in color #232
3. Swarovski 5 mm crystals in Siam
4. Focal beads by Winterglass

45-Inch Lariat Made with #9 Three-cut Beads

Beginning to Work with Patterns

The next several "bangle" projects have different patterns and will give you a hands-on feel of how patterns emerge. Further, you will be using the smallest of the yarns recommended in this book. (If you find this size yarn difficult to use, and you would prefer not to use it, the bangles can be made using #20 weight crochet cotton. However, if you would like to give yourself the greatest flexibility in your own bead crochet designs, give this weight yarn a chance.)

Project 4
Zigzag Bangle

Materials and Tools Needed

7.5 grams #11 seed beads (Color A)
4 grams #11 seed beads (Color B)
2 grams #11 seed beads (Color C)
#30 weight crochet cotton
Size 9 (1.25 mm) or 10 (1.15 mm) crochet hook
Thin tapestry needle or #10 beading needle
Silamide to match (if you elect to attach the tube in that manner, described in the "Tips" chapter of this book)

Stringing Sequence 1: 4A 1B 1C 1B
Stringing Sequence 2: 5A 1B 1C 1B

Load Sequence 1 five times, followed by Sequence 2 five times. Continue to load in this manner until you have loaded 3 to 5 feet of beads.

Crochet 7 around until your bangle measures 7 inches, or the desired length. Block your work. Attach one end of the tube to the other using any of the methods described in Chapter 2.

For this project, I used:
1. Miyuki size #11 seed beads in colors #30, #11, and #193
2. Cébélia® #30 weight crochet cotton in color #816

Four Patterned Bangles

Project 5
Broken Lines Bangle

Materials and Tools Needed

7.5 grams #11 seed beads (Color A)
7.5 grams #11 seed beads (Color B)
#30 weight crochet cotton
Size 9 (1.25 mm) or 10 (1.15 mm) crochet
    hook
Big "Eye" needle
Thin tapestry needle
#10 beading needles
 Silamide to match

Stringing Sequence 1:
    ROW 1: 1A 1B 1A 1B 1A 1B 1A 1B
    ROW 2: 9A

Stringing Sequence 2:
    ROW 1: 1A 1B 1A 1B 1A 1B 1A 1B
    ROW 2: 9B

Using the Big "Eye" needle, string 12 to 14 inches of Sequence 1 and crochet 8 around for 1.75 inches. Tie off yarn. String 25 to 28 inches of Sequence 2 and crochet 8 around for 3.75 inches. Tie off yarn. String another 12 to 14 inches of Sequence 1 and crochet 8 around for another 1.75 inches. Tie off yarn. Block your work. Using either method described in Chapter 2, join one end of the tube to the other.

For this project I used:
1. Miyuki #11 seed bead in color #574
2. #11 seed beads in color #30, available from Jane's Fiber & Beads
3. Cébélia® #30 weight crochet cotton in color #799

Project 6
Broken Spiral Bangle

Materials and Tools Needed

10 grams #11 seed beads in color A
2.5 grams (each) of #11 seed beads in colors
    B, C, D, E
#30 weight crochet cotton
Size 9 (1.25 mm) or 10 (1.15 mm) crochet
    hook
Big "Eye" needle
Two thin tapestry needles
One larger decorative connecting bead

Stringing Sequence:
    ROW 1: 1A 1B 1A 1C 1A 1D 1A 1E
    ROW 2: 8A

Leaving a long tail (8 to 10 inches) of yarn at the beginning, bead chain 8 stitches using the sequence above. Crochet 8 around for 6.5 to 7 inches (or desired length). Tie off yarn, leaving a long tail (8 to 10 inches). Thread each tail onto a thin tapestry needle (or #10 beading needle). Pass the two needles through the decorative bead in opposite directions. Pass each needle through a stitch in the end row. Take the needle and run it up the center of the tube about 1/2 inch, and come out through one side of the tube. Then take your needle and pass it through the tube on the perpendicular. Pass the needle back down the center of the tube and back through the decorative bead. Repeat until the joining feels very secure. (See the "Tips" chapter of this book for a more detailed explanation of this attachment technique.)

For this project, I used:
1. Miyuki #11 seed beads colors #401SF, #4, #10, #17, and #20
2. A Paula Radke dichroic bead for the connecting bead
3. Cébélia® #30 weight crochet cotton in color #310

Project 7
Large Diamond Bangle

Materials and Tools Needed

7.5 grams #11 seed beads in color A
2.5 grams #11 seed beads in color B
#30 weight crochet cotton
Size 9 (1.25 mm) or 10 (1.15 mm) crochet hook
Big "Eye" needle
Thin tapestry needle
#10 beading needles
Silamide to match

Stringing Sequence:
    ROW 1: 1B 7A
    ROW 2: 2B 6A
    ROW 3: 1B 1A 1B 5A
    ROW 4: 1B 2A 1B 4A
    ROW 5: 1B 3A 1B 3A
    ROW 6: 1B 4A 1B 2A
    ROW 7: 1B 5A 1B 1A
    ROW 8: 1B 6A 1B

Load 3 to 6 feet of beads using the eight-row sequence given above, and crochet 8 around until the tube measures 7 inches or desired length. (You may have to tie off and load additional beads.) Block your work. Attach the tube to itself using one of the methods described in Chapter 2.

For this project I used:
1. #11 seed beads in colors #636 and #F16a, available from Jane's Fiber & Beads
2. Cébélia® #30 weight crochet cotton in color #745

Project 8
Silver Flowered Necklace

I used silver spacers for most of this project, instead of #11 seed beads. I was hoping that doing so would give you additional ideas for your own bead crochet projects. I also used Hill Tribe silver flowers to enhance the design and connected them in a way as to allow some "movement" of the flowers when worn. The pattern is not difficult, but is given a slightly different look by crocheting 7 around (as opposed to an even number), and the spacing between the patterns is also an uneven number of rows. Since the silver is heavier than glass beads, be careful to pull out all the excess stretch when blocking or your piece will "grow" when you wear it.

Materials and Tools Needed

Four 16-inch strands of 2 mm faceted Hill Tribe silver spacers (Color A) (or any other spacers that you like that are approximately 2 mm)
2 grams #11 seed beads (Color B)
Two small Hill Tribe silver flowers (approximately 1/2 inch across)
One large Hill Tribe silver flower (approximate 1 inch across)
Six flat Bali spacers
#30 weight crochet cotton
Size 9 (1.25 mm) or 10 (1.15 mm) crochet hook
Big "Eye" needle
Two thin tapestry needles
#10 beading needles
Two bead caps or cones
Clasp
Two 3-inch eyepins or 6 inches of 20 to 22 gauge wire, cut in half
Chain nose pliers
Round nose pliers
Wire cutters
Scissors

Stringing Sequence 1:
　　1A 1B 1A 1B 1A 1B 1A
Stringing Sequence 2:
　　21 A
Stringing Sequence 3:
　　2A 1B 1A 1B 1A 1B 1A

Varying the number of times you string sequence 1 and 3 between two and five times, load as follows:

Sequence 1 (two to five times)
Sequence 2 (one time)
Sequence 3 (two to five times)
Sequence 2 (one time)

Crochet 7 around for the entire piece.

Crochet two pieces that are 6 inches, and two pieces that are 2.5 inches (or desired length). In each case, do one final round of beadless chains, decreasing 3 stitches in that last round. Block the pieces well.

Attachment: Using the tail of #30 weight yarn (or attaching a new 15-inch piece of yarn to one of the 6-inch pieces and a new piece of yarn to one of the 2.5-inch pieces), thread the yarn onto a #10 beading needle. (If you are unable to thread the yarn, use the thinnest tapestry needle you can find.) Pick up a flat spacer and one of the faceted Hill Tribe silver beads with each of the needles. Then pass each of the needles through one of the smaller flowers, and through the two silver beads and spacers on the opposite needle. Pass each of the needles about 1/2 inch up into the opposite tube, and pull the thread tight. Cross the tube on the perpendicular. Pass the needle back down the tube, into both spacers, through the flower, through the two spacers on the opposite side, and back up into the tube (about 1/2 inch). Anchor the thread, and pass the needle through the tube on the perpendicular. Repeat with each needle as many times as necessary to secure the two tubes together.

Do the same thing with the other 6-inch and 2.5-inch crocheted tubes. After you have completed that, join your two sides in the middle, in the same way, using the larger flower.

Sew the eyepins to each end of the tube as described in the preceding projects. Thread a bead cap or cone over the wire, and connect the wire to the clasp using a wrapped loop.

For this project, I used:
1. Four 16-inch strands of 2 mm faceted Hill Tribe silver spacers
2. Miyuki #11 seed beads in color #401F
3. Six Turkish flower spacers
4. Three Hill Tribe silver flowers in two sizes
5. Two Bali cones
6. Cébélia® #30 weight crochet cotton in color #762
7. One lobster claw clasp

Silver Flowered Necklace

Project 9
Using Two Different
Bead Sizes within the Piece

This project is designed to help you begin using different sizes of beads in the same piece. The way that this pattern is constructed maximizes some of the problems of changing sizes while minimizing the attention needed to other things (such as a complex stringing sequence). Should you find this crocheting particularly difficult, try the project using #20 weight crochet cotton before you use #30 weight crochet cotton. You may find that you have "recessed" beads where a smaller bead sits next to a larger bead. Prior to pulling out your work, try inserting a size #1 knitting needle into the tube and to see if it forces the recessed bead to pop out.

Materials and Tools Needed

20 grams #8 seed beads (Color B)
17.5 grams #11 seed beads (Color A)
#30 weight crochet cotton
Size 9 (1.25 mm) or 10 (1.15 mm) crochet hook
Two 3-inch eyepins or 6 inches of 20 to 22 gauge wire, cut in half
Two end caps or cones
Clasp
Round nose pliers
Chain nose pliers
Wire cutters
Scissors

Stringing sequence:
    ROW 1: 1A 1B 1A 1B 1A 1B 1A 1B
    ROW 2: 8A

Load 3 to 5 feet of beads using the two-row sequence given above. Crochet 8 around until the necklace is 22 inches or desired length. Do one final round of beadless chains, decreasing 3 stitches in this last round. Block your work.

Sew the eyepins or wire to the ends of the tube as described in the earlier projects. Thread the bead cap or cone over the wire, and attach the clasp with a wrapped loop.

For this project, I used:
1. Miyuki #8 seed beads in color #188
2. Toho #11 seed beads in color #461
3. Cébélia® #30 weight crochet cotton in color #841
4. Two Hill Tribe vermeil tulip bead caps
5. Vermeil clasp

Using Two
Different
Bead Sizes
within the
Piece

29

Project 10
Black and White Lariat

Black and White Lariat

This project was designed to give you a taste of various techniques and patterns. The end of the lariat is made using sculptural crochet and is attached to lampwork beads with fringe. There are different patterns throughout the lariat. If the instructions seem overwhelming to you, pick one sequence and make a bracelet or necklace using just that one.

Materials and Tools Needed

One hank white opaque #9 three-cut beads (Color A)
One hank black opaque #9 three-cut beads (Color B)
5 grams semi-matte #11 black seed beads (Color C)
2 grams white opaque small cylinder beads (Color D)
5 grams white opaque #8 seed beads (Color E)
5 grams black opaque #8 seed beads (Color F)
1 gram red silver-lined matte #11 seed beads (Color G)
1 gram blue silver-lined matte #11 seed beads (Color H)
1 gram purple silver-lined matte #11 seed beads (Color I)
Twenty-four 4 mm bicone crystals in chalk white (Color J)
Twelve 6 mm faceted crystals in jet black (Color K)
#30 weight crochet cotton
Size 9 (1.25 mm) or 10 (1.15 mm) crochet hook
Silamide to match
#10 beading needles
Big "Eye" needle
Thin tapestry needle
Two large (approximately 14 to 16 mm) decorative beads
Scissors
One pipe cleaner

Stringing Sequence 1:
  2D 1B 1E 1F 2A 1C

Load Sequence 1 repeatedly and crochet 8 around for 4.5 inches.

Stringing Sequence 2:
  6B 2A

Load Sequence 2 repeatedly and crochet 8 around for 6 inches .

Stringing Sequence 3:
  ROW 1: 8A
  ROW 2: 8B
  ROWS 3-4: Repeat ROW 1
  ROWS 5-6: Repeat ROW 2
  ROWS 6-8: Repeat ROW 1
  ROWS 9-11: Repeat ROW 2
  ROWS 12-15: Repeat ROW 1
  ROWS 16-19: Repeat ROW 2
  ROWS 20-22: Repeat ROW 1
  ROWS 23-25: Repeat ROW 2
  ROWS 26-27: Repeat ROW 1
  ROWS 28-29: Repeat ROW 2
  ROW 30: Repeat ROW 1
  ROW 31: Repeat ROW 2

Load Rows 1 through 31 and crochet 8 around.

Stringing Sequence 4:
  ROW 1: 8A
  ROW 2: 1A 1C 1A 1C 1A 1C 1A 1C
  ROW 3: 9A

Load Row 1 once, and then Rows 2 and 3 (alternating between the two) repeatedly. Crochet 8 around for 1.5 inches

Stringing Sequence 5:
  ROW 1: 7A 1B
  ROW 2: 6A 2B
  ROW 3: 5A 3B
  ROW 4: 4A 4B
  ROW 5: 3A 2B 1G 2B
  ROW 6: 2A 2B 2G 2B
  ROW 7: 1A 2B 3G 2B
  ROW 8: 2B 4G 2B
  ROW 9: 2B 3G 2B 1A
  ROW 10: 2B 2G 2B 2A
  ROW 11: 2B 1G 2B 3A
  ROW 12: 4B 4A
  ROW 13: 3B 5A
  ROW 14: 2B 6A
  ROW 15: 1B 7A
  ROW 16: 8A

Load Rows 1 through 16 and crochet 8 around.

Repeat Rows 1 through 16 substituting H for G.
Repeat Rows 1 through16 substituting I for G.

Sequence 6:
  Repeat Sequence 4

Stringing Sequence 7:
ROW 1: 8A
ROW 2: 3A 2B 1A 2B

Load Row 1 once, then Row 2 repeatedly, and crochet 8 around for 3 inches.

Stringing Sequence 8:
ROW 1: 8B
ROW 2: 1B 1A 1B 1A 1B 1A 1B 1A
ROW 3: 9B

Load Row 1 once, then Rows 2 and 3 (alternating between the two) repeatedly. Crochet 8 around for 2.25 inches.

Sequence 9:
Repeat Sequence 7

Sequence 10:
Repeat Sequence 4

Sequence 11:
Repeat Sequence 5

Sequence 12:
Repeat Sequence 4

Sequence 13:
Repeat Sequence 3

Sequence 14:
Repeat Sequence 2

Sequence 15:
Repeat Sequence 1, but only for 2.5 inches.

Fringe: Thread an 18-inch piece of #30 weight crochet cotton through a #10 beading needle and make a small knot at the end. Thread 4 yards of Silamide on a #10 beading needle and pull the ends even, doubling the thread. (You'll be using doubled thread for the fringe.) Make a small knot at the very end. Anchor both the yarn and the Silamide in the center of the tube at one end. Take both needles and pass them through your "end" bead. If the hole in your end bead is large enough for a #11 seed bead to slip into, plug the hole with a pipe cleaner.

Using the yarn first, pick up 15A 1J 5B 3A 1K 3A 5B 1J 15A, then pass the needle back through your end bead and anchor the yarn in the tube. Pass the needle and yarn across the tube on the perpendicular to secure it. Using the second needle threaded with Silamide, pick up the same sequence as you did with the yarn. Pass the needle and thread back through the end bead, and anchor it in your tube. Repeat the same sequence for the next fringe.

To make the fourth fringe, substitute any two of the above beads with G, spaced away from each other and randomly. Do the same with the fifth fringe, substituting H for any two beads. Repeat with I. Make sure that your fringe is holding the end bead to the lariat securely. If it isn't, using only one strand of Silamide, pass your needle and thread through the fringe a second time, securing it further up into the tube. Repeat with a single strand of Silamide as needed. Make the same eight strands of fringe on the other end of your lariat.

For this project I used:
1. Czech opaque white #9 three-cut beads
2. Czech opaque black #9 three-cut beads
3. All of the white seed beads are Miyuki beads color #402
4. All of the black seed beads are Miyuki beads color #401
5. Matsuno #11 seed beads in colors #084m, #071m, and #041m
6. Miyuki Delicas™ in color #200
7. #30 weight Cébélia® crochet cotton in color #5200
8. Swarovski crystals
9. Focal beads by Silver Cloud Trading Company

Project 11
Sculptural Necklace
with Lampwork Beads

In this project you will learn to make an extraordinarily sculptural necklace that also incorporates lampwork beads. To get the "undulating" effect, the size of the beads must change fairly dramatically. In this piece, you'll notice that the beads range from small cylinders to #8 seed beads. If you wish to get an even greater sculptural effect, use size #15 seed beads as well as #6 seed beads in addition to the beads used in this project.

Materials and Tools Needed

7 grams small cylinders (Color A)
4 grams small cylinders (Color B)
10 grams size #11 seed beads (Color C)
6 grams size #11 seed beads (Color D)
6 grams size #11 seed beads (Color E)
12 grams size #8 seed beads (Color F)
12 grams size #8 seed beads (Color G)
#30 weight crochet cotton
Size 9 (1.25 mm) or 10 (1.15 mm) crochet hook
Big "Eye" needle
Two thin tapestry needles
#10 beading needles
Two 3-inch eyepins or 6 inches of 20 to 22 gauge wire, cut in half
Two bead caps or cones
Clasp
One or more lampwork beads
Round nose pliers
Chain nose pliers
Wire cutters
Scissors

Stringing Sequence to be used throughout the project:

2A 1B 1C 1D 1F 1G 1E 1D

Crochet 9 around for the entire project.

Crochet two pieces that are 8 inches each and one piece that is 12 inches (or desired lengths). In the final round of each piece, do one round of beadless chains, decreasing 4 stitches in that round. Block your work. Connect the two 8-inch pieces to a lampwork bead using two thin tapestry needles, as described in the "Tips" chapter of this book. Attach one end of one of the 8-inch pieces to the 12-inch piece with two spacers and one lampwork bead, again using the two tapestry needles. (Refer back to the "Tips" chapter as needed.)

Attach the two eyepins or wire as described in earlier projects. Thread one bead cap or cone over each piece of wire, and attach to the clasp with a wrapped loop.

For this project, I used:
1. Miyuki Delicas™ in colors #101 and #709
2. Miyuki #11 seed beads in colors #132, #132F, and #135
3. Miyuki #8 seed beads in colors #134 and #134F
4. Cébélia® crochet cotton in color #437
5. Hill Tribe silver bead caps
6. A clasp from Scottsdale Bead Supply
7. Lampwork beads by Kathy Perras/Itzart

Sculptural Necklace
with Lampwork Beads

Project 12
Centered Focal Bead
with Crocheted Bail

Centered Focal Bead with Crocheted Bail

In this necklace, you will learn a new pattern as well as how to crochet a bail. This will enable you to hang a focal bead vertically, giving you a new way to show off that bead. Further, the bead "caps" are made using #15 seed beads. It may be a touch that you would like to have in your "arsenal."

Materials and Tools Needed

6 grams small cylinder beads (Color A)
8 grams #11 seed beads (Color B)
8 grams #11 seed beads (Color C)
6 grams #11 seed beads in (Color D)
12 grams #8 seed beads in (Color E)
2 grams #15 seed beads in any matching color
#30 weight crochet cotton
Size 9 (1.25 mm) or 10 (1.15 mm) crochet hook
Big "Eye" needle
Thin tapestry needle
#10 and/or #12 beading needles
Silamide to match
Assorted fringe beads, including crystals
Focal bead
Two 3-inch eyepins or 6 inches of 20 to 22 gauge wire, cut in half
Round nose pliers
Chain nose pliers
Wire cutters
Scissors

Stringing Sequence:
ROW 1: 1D 1E 1D 2B 3C
ROW 2: 1A 1D 1E 1D 1B 3C
ROW 3: 2A 1D 1E 1D 3C
ROW 4: 3A 1D 1E 1D 2C
ROW 5: 3A 1B 1D 1E 1D 1C
ROW 6: 3A 2B 1D 1E 1D
ROW 7: 3A 2B 1C 1D 1E
ROW 8: 1D 2A 2B 2C 1D
ROW 9: 1E 1D 1A 2B 3C

Load 3 to 5 feet of beads following the stringing sequence above. Crochet 8 around until your piece measures 9 inches (or desired length). In the next round, do 4 beadless slip stitches, followed by 4 beaded slip stitches. In the last round, decrease 2 stitches on the "beadless" side, followed by 4 beaded slip stitches. Tie off yarn and block.

Make a second tube identical to the first.

Attach a new yarn to one of the tubes as you normally would. Holding the two tubes together with the beadless sides touching each other, bead crochet 8 around using the four beaded slip stitches on each of the tubes until your new "married" tube measures 1/2 inch or desired length. Thread two #10 beading needles with #30 weight crochet cotton and two #10 beading needles with Silamide. Anchor all four needles in the tube, and pull all four through your focal bead. Make a fringe using each strand of yarn and each strand of Silamide, securing two of them approximately 1/2 inch up in each of the original tubes you crocheted. Repeat with the Silamide two to four times, depending upon how much fringe you want. Check to make sure that your focal bead is secure.

In this project, you can make your own bead caps, should you desire, using #15 seed beads. Thread a #10 or #12 beading needle with 2.5 to 3 yards of Silamide. Pull the ends so that one end is 8 inches shorter than the other. Pick up eight #15 seed beads with your needle. Leaving a 6-inch tail, take your needle and pass it through the same beads in the same direction, forming a small circle. Pull the thread tight and maintain a tight tension for Rounds #1 through #7.

Round #1: Pick up two more beads, go through the next two beads, and pick up two more beads. Again, go through the next two beads, pick up two beads and go through the next two beads. You will pick up four pairs of beads in this round.

Round #2: Begin the round with a step-up. Pull the shorter end of the thread so that it is 1 inch past the step up. You will start working with a doubled thread at this time, and you should complete the cap using doubled thread. Pass the needle up through the first bead of the first pair added in Round #1. Pick up two beads and exit down through the second bead of the first pair in Round #1. Pick up one bead, then pass the needle up through the first bead of the second pair added in Round #1. Repeat around, adding a total of 4 pairs with one "in-fill" bead between each pair.

Round #3: Begin the round with a step-up. Do exactly as you did in Round #2, but add two beads between each pair, for a total of 16 beads, four pairs in the original stacks and four pairs of "in-fill" beads.

Rounds #4 through #6: Begin the round with a step-up. Pass the needle up through the first bead of the first pair. Pick up two beads. Pass the needle down through the second bead of that pair. Pass the needle up through the first "in-fill" bead. Pick up two beads and pass the needle down through the second "in-fill" bead. Repeat around for a total of 16 beads per round, which will be composed of eight pairs of beads. (Note: Your cap will become a "cup" in about the fifth or sixth round, so if it's flat until then, don't assume that you are doing it incorrectly.)

Round #7: Repeat Round #6, but add one "in-fill" bead between each pair of beads, for a total of 24 beads, which will be composed of eight pairs and eight in-fill beads.

Round #8: Pass the needle up through the first bead of the first pair. Add one bead in the center of the pair, and pass the needle down through the second bead of that pair. Repeat around.

Finishing: Reinforce the cap by passing your needle and thread up and down each stack, using a vertical thread path. Trim the thread tails off.

Attach an eyepin or piece of wire to end of each of the tubes as you did in previous projects, and then feed your beaded bead cap over each eyepin or wire. Feed one #8 seed bead over the wire and hold it tightly against the cap. Attach the clasp using a wrapped loop.

NOTE: If you want to make a bead cap that is the right size for a tube crocheted with size #11 seed beads and #30 weight crochet cotton, eliminate Round #7.

For this project, I used:
1. Miyuki Delicas™ in color #110
2. #11 seed beads in colors #F356B and #430i, available from Jane's Fiber & Beads
3. Miyuki #11 seed beads in color #1089
4. #8 seed beads in color #141a, available from Jane's Fiber & Beads
5. #15 seed beads in color #430i, available from Jane's Fiber & Beads
6. Cébélia® #30 weight crochet cotton in color # 524
7. Clasp from Scottsdale Bead Supply
8. Lampwork bead by Nancy Tobey

Project 13 (A and B)
Dimensional Diamonds

This is a more difficult stringing sequence, but as soon as you start crocheting, the pattern can be seen easily. I made two versions of this project with two different sizes and shapes of beads so that you could see just how different they look depending upon which beads you choose. You can also make this pattern using only #11 seed beads if you prefer the necklace without any additional dimension. In short, this is a pattern that lends itself to many variations with just a little alteration to the pattern below, and each time you vary it, the end result will look surprisingly different.

Dimensional Diamonds 32-Inch Necklace (A)

Materials and Tools Needed

15 grams #11cut seed beads (Color A)
10 grams #11 seed beads (Color B)
10 grams #11 seed beads (Color C)
6 grams small cylinder beads (Color D)
6 grams small cylinder beads (Color E)
#30 weight crochet cotton
Size 9 (1.25) crochet hook
Two 3-inch eyepins or 6 inches of 20 to 22 gauge wire, cut in half
Two bead caps or cones
Clasp
Round nose pliers
Chain nose pliers
Wire cutters
Scissors

Dimensional Diamonds 18-Inch Necklace (B)

Materials and Tools Needed

17.5 grams #8 seed beads (Color A)
10 grams #11 seed beads (Color B)
6 grams small cylinder beads (Color C)
10 grams #11 seed beads (Color D)
6 grams small cylinder beads (Color E)
#30 weight crochet cotton
Same tools and findings as above

Stringing Sequence:
ROW 1: 1A 2B 3C 2B
ROW 2: 2A 2B 2C 2B
ROW 3: 1A 1D 1A 2B 1C 2B
ROW 4: 1A 2D 1A 4B
ROW 5: 1A 3D 1A 3B
ROW 6: 1A 4D 1A 2B
ROW 7: 1A 2D 1E 2D 1A 1B
ROW 8: 1A 2D 2E 2D 1A
ROW 9: 1A 2D 3E 2D
ROW 10: 2A 2D 2E 2D
ROW 11: 1A 1B 1A 2D 1E 2D
ROW 12: 1A 2B 1A 4D
ROW 13: 1A 3B 1A 3D
ROW 14: 1A 4B 1A 2D
ROW 15: 1A 2B 1C 2B 1A 1D
ROW 16: 1A 2B 2C 2B 1A

Load according to pattern above and crochet 8 around until you reach desired length. Do one final round of beadless chains, decreasing 3 stitches in that round. Block your work. Using a chain nose pliers, close the loop of the eyepin until the wires touch. (Instead of an eyepin, you may choose to use wire with a small loop made in one end.) Sew the eyepins to each end of the tube. Thread a bead cap or cone over each eyepin. Hold the cap (or cone) firmly against the tube, and connect the clasp to the eyepins using a wrapped loop.

For the Dimensional Diamonds 32-Inch project, I used:
1. Miyuki #11cut seed beads in color #191F (Color A)
2. Matsuno #11 seed beads in color #68M (Color B)
3. Miyuki Delicas™ in color #2002 (Color C)
4. Matusno #11 seed beads in color #084m (Color D)
5. Miyuki Delicas™ in color #230 (Color E)
6. Cébélia® #30 weight crochet cotton in Color #816
7. Clasp fom Star's Clasps

For the Dimensional Diamond Necklace 18-Inch project, I used:
1. Miyuki #8 seed beads in color #187 (Color A)

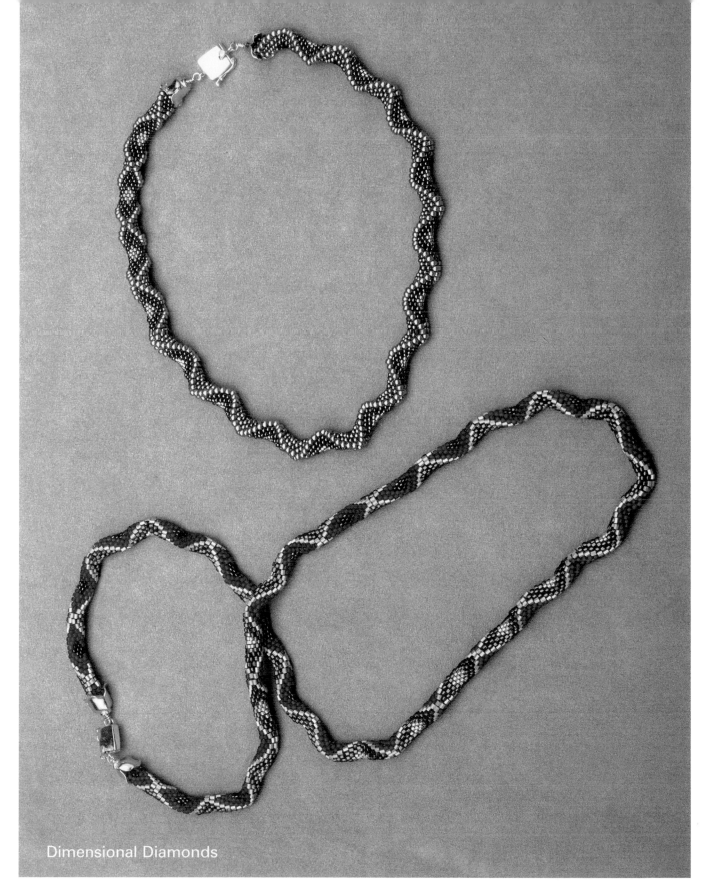

Dimensional Diamonds

2. Toho #11 seed beads in color #222 (Color B)

3. Miyuki Delicas™ in color #508 (Color C)

4. #11 seed beads in color #460i, available from Jane's Fiber & Beads (Color D)

5. Miyuki Delicas™ in color #11(cut) (Color E)

6. Cébélia® #30 weight crochet cotton in color #524

7. Clasp from Star's Clasps

Project 14
Overlapping Spirals

This is a very complex stringing pattern. I suggest that you find both a comfortable and foolproof method of stringing. (There are a number of suggestions in the "Tips" chapter of this book.) Double check your work while you are stringing, as it can be difficult to find exactly where in the sequence you are if you make a stringing error.

Materials and Tools Needed:

20 grams #10 twisted hex beads (Color A)
12 grams #8 seed beads (Color B)
8 grams #11 seed beads (Color C)
5 grams small cylinder beads (Color D)
8 grams #11 seed beads (Color E)
12 grams #8 seed beads (Color F)
5 grams small cylinder beads (Color G)
#30 weight crochet cotton
Size 9 (1.25 mm) or 10 (1.15 mm) crochet hook
Two 3-inch eyepins or 6 inches of 20 to 22 gauge wire, cut in half
Two bead caps or cones
Clasp
Round nose pliers
Chain nose pliers
Wire cutter
Scissors

Stringing Sequence (for the pattern used throughout this project):
ROW 1: 1A 1B 1A 1C 4D
ROW 2: 1E 1A 1B 1A 1C 3D
ROW 3: 1E 2A 1B 1A 1C 2D
ROW 4: 1E 1A 1F 1A 1B 1A 1C 1D
ROW 5: 1E 1A 1F 2A 1B 1A 1C
ROW 6: 1E 1A 1F 1A 1G 1A 1B 1A
ROW 7: 1E 1A 1F 1A 2G 1A 1B
ROW 8: 1E 1A 1F 1A 3G 1A
ROW 9: 1E 1A 1F 1A 4G
ROW 10: 1E 1A 1F 1A 4G
ROW 11: 1E 1A 1F 1A 1C 3G
ROW 12: 1E 1A 1F 2A 1C 2G
ROW 13: 1E 1A 1F 1A 1B 1A 1C 1G

ROW 14: 1E 1A 1F 2A 1B 1A 1C
ROW 15: 1E 1A 1F 1A 1D 1A 1B 1A
ROW 16: 1C 1A 1F 1A 2D 1A 1B
ROW 17: 1A 1C 1F 1A 3D 1A
ROW 18: 1B 1A 1C 1A 4D

CODE to assist you when stringing:
A = #10 twisted hex (Color A)
B = #8 seed bead (Color B)
C = #11 seed bead (Color C)
D = small cylinder (Color D)
E = #11 seed bead (Color E)
F = #8 seed bead (Color F)
G = small cylinder (Color G)

Load 3 to 5 feet following the stringing sequence described above. (Make sure to string complete sequences.) Crochet 8 around for 17 inches or desired length. Do one round of beadless chain stitches, decreasing 3 stitches in that round. Block your work. (Be careful not to over-block this piece or the 'wiggle' will come out.) Sew in the eyepins (or 22 gauge wire) as described in previous projects. Feed bead cap or cone over the eyepin and attach clasp with a wrapped loop.

For this project, I used:
1. Miyuki #10 twisted hex in color #462 (Color A)
2. Miyuki #8 seed beads in color #460 (Color B)
3. Miyuki #11 seed beads in color #457 (Color C)
4. Miyuki Delicas™ in color #12(cut) (Color D)
5. Miyuki #11 seed beads in color #460 (Color E)
6. Miyuki #8 seed beads in color #457 (Color F)
7. Miyuki Delicas™ in color #22(cut) (Color G)
8. Cébélia® #30 weight crochet cotton in color #816
9. Hill Tribe silver tulip bead caps
10. Vermeil clasp

Overlapping Spirals

Project 15
Drop Lariat

This project was constructed in a manner similar to the black and white lariat (Project 10), in that it is a sampler of many different patterns. In this case, almost all of the sequences utilize drops. Again, if the instructions seem intimidating, try selecting one sequence that appeals to you and make a bracelet or shorter necklace before attempting this entire lariat.

Materials and Tools needed:

30 grams drops (Color A) [DP]
15 grams #11 seed beads (Color A)
6 grams #11 seed beads (Color B)
6 grams #11 seed beads (Color C)
6 grams #11 seed beads (Color D)
6 grams #11 seed beads (Color E)
5 grams bugles (Color A)
#30 weight crochet cotton
Size 9 crochet hook (1.25 mm)
Silamide to match
#10 beading needles
Big "Eye" needle

Note: You will be crocheting 8 around for this entire project.

Stringing Sequence 1:
    ROW 1: 8 DP
    ROW 2: 8A

Load a total of 28 rows of Sequence 1, and then load another 8A to finish loading this sequence. Your last two rows loaded will both be 8A. Crochet 8 around.

Stringing Sequence 2: Load each row three times before loading the next row.
    ROW 1: 3C 2B 3A
    ROW 2: 4C 1B 3A
    ROW 3: 5C 3A
    ROW 4: 6C 2A
    ROW 5: 7C 1A
    ROW 6: 8C

Crochet 8 around for a total of 18 rows.

Stringing Sequence 3:
    3C 2B 3A

Crochet 8 around until lariat measures about 10.5 inches.

Stringing Sequence 4:
    ROW 1: 1DP 3A 1DP 3A
    ROW 2: 9A
    ROWS 3-4: Repeat Rows 1 and 2
    ROW 5: 1DP 3E 1DP 3E
    ROW 6: 9E
    ROWS 7-8: Repeat Rows 5 and 6
    ROWS 9-10: Repeat Rows 1 and 2
    ROWS 11-14: Repeat Rows 5-8
    ROWS 15-16: Repeat Rows 1 and 2
    ROWS 17-20: Repeat Row 5-8 using Color C
    ROWS 21-22: Repeat Rows 1 and 2
    ROWS 23-26: Repeat Rows 5-8 using Color D
    ROWS 27-28: Repeat Rows 1 and 2
    ROWS 29-32: Repeat Rows 5-8 using Color B
    ROWS 33-34: Repeat Rows 1 and 2
    ROWS 35-38: Repeat Rows 5-8 using Color D
    ROWS 39-40: Repeat Rows 1 and 2
    ROWS 41-44: Repeat Rows 5-8 using Color C
    ROWS 45-46: Repeat Rows 1 and 2
    ROWS 47-50: Repeat Rows 5-8 using Color E
    ROWS 51-52: Repeat Rows 1 and 2
    ROWS 53-56: Repeat Rows 5-8 using Color B
    ROWS 57-58: Repeat Rows 1 and 2
    ROWS 59-62: Repeat Rows 5-8 using Color C

Crochet 8 around for one full sequence (Rows 1 through 62).

Drop Lariat

Stringing Sequence 5:
ROW 1: 1DP 1A 1DP 1D 2B 2E
ROW 2: 1C 3A 2B 2E
ROW 3: 2C 1DP 1A 1DP 1B 2E
ROW 4: 2C 1D 3A 2E
ROW 5: 2C 2D 1DP 1A 1DP 1E
ROW 6: 2C 2D 1E 3A
ROW 7: 2C 2D 2E 1DP 1A
ROW 8: 1DP 1C 2D 2B 1E 1A
ROW 9: 1A 1DP 2D 2B 2E

Crochet 8 around for 5 inches.

Stringing Sequence 6:
ROWS 1-8: 8A
ROW 9: 8DP
ROWS 10-17: 8D
ROW 18: 8DP
ROW 19-22: 8A
ROW 23: 8DP
ROWS 24-31: 8B
ROW 32: 8DP
ROWS 33-36: 8A
ROW 37: 8DP
ROWS 38-45: 8E
ROW 46: 8DP
ROWS 47-50: 8A
ROW 48: 8DP
ROWS 49-56: 8C
ROW 57: 8DP
ROWS 58-65: 8A

Crochet 8 around for one entire sequence (Rows 1 through 65).

Stringing Sequence 7:
ROW 1: 1C 1A 1D 1A 1B 1A 1E 1A
ROW 2: 1C 1DP 1D 1DP 1B 1DP 1E 1DP

Crochet 8 around for 4.5 inches.

Stringing Sequence 8:
ROW 1: 6D 3A
ROW 2: 6D 1DP 1A 1DP
String Rows 1 and 2 consecutively 6 times (for a total of 12 rows)
ROW 3: 5D 3A
ROW 4: 5D 1A 1DP 1A
String Rows 3 and 4 consecutively 6 times (for a total of 12 rows)

Repeat this entire sequence (total of 24 rows), substituting Color B. Repeat again using Color C, then again with Color E.

Crochet 8 around for all four colors.

Stringing Sequence 9:
ROW 1: 3C 2B 3A

Load this row repeatedly and crochet 8 around for an additional 8.5 inches.

Stringing Sequence 10:
ROWS 1-3: 3C 2B 3A
ROWS 4-6: 4C 1B 3A
ROWS 5-7: 5C 3A
ROWS 8-10: 6C 2A
ROWS 11-13: 7C 1A
ROWS 14-16: 8C

Crochet 8 around for a total of 16 rows.

Stringing Sequence 11:
Load 16A, then,
ROW 1: 8A
ROW 2: 8DP

Load Rows 1 and 2 consecutively 14 times (a total of 28 rows), and crochet 8 around.

Block completed lariat before adding fringe.

Adding fringe: Using Silamide and #10 beading needles, anchor the thread into one of the #11 seed beads in the exterior row (of your initial two rows). Then pick up 8A, 1 bugle, 2A, 1 bugle, 2A, and one drop. Use the drop as a pivot bead, and run your needle and thread back up the other beads you just picked up. Anchor the thread in the next #11 seed bead, and repeat for the next fringe. Repeat around the entire exterior row, adding a total of eight fringes. If you like a fuller fringe, continue to add as desired using the interior row of #11 seed beads.

For this project I used:
1. Miyuki drops, seed beads and bugles in color #401 FR
2. Miyuki #11 seed beads in colors #460, #457, and #467
3. #11 seed beads in colors #430i and #F374D, available from Jane's Fiber & Beads
4. Cébélia® #30 weight crochet cotton in color #932

Resources

For each item listed below, a phone number and web address (or other address) will be provided the first time the source is mentioned and will not be repeated. If you cannot find an item listed under a particular project or section, look for it in an earlier project or section. For example, if a source for Miyuki beads is given under Project 1, it will not be repeated. If you're looking at Project 10 and can't find the Miyuki beads that you're looking for, look for them in the earlier projects.

Yarns listed in Tools of the Trade

Opera yarns available from Handy Hands, in both wholesale and retail quantities. Phone: 217-379-3802. Web address: www.hhtatting.com.

Flora yarns available from Handy Hands, both wholesale and retail. Also available from Lacis in both wholesale and retail quantities. Phone: 510-843-7178. Web address: www.lacis.com.

DMC Cébélia® yarn available from Handy Hands, and from Lacis.

DMC Perle cotton available from Handy Hands.

Fincrochet by Presencia available from Bag Lady Press, in both wholesale and retail quantities. Phone: 1-888-222-4523. Web address: www.baglady.com.

Finca Perle cotton (a Presencia product) available from Bag Lady Press.

Project 1

Miyuki beads available from Caravan Beads in Portland, Maine, in both wholesale and retail quantities. Phone: 1-800-230-8941. Web address: www.caravanbeads.com.

Bali bead caps available from Rishashay. Phone: 1-800-517-3311. Web address: www.rishashay.com. Also available from Singaraja Imports. Phone: 1-800-865-8856. Web address: www.singarajaimports.com.

Clasp available from Pegasus Imports. Phone: 1-800-742-bead. Address: 4455 Hall Road, Santa Rosa, CA 95401.

Project 2

Toho beads available from The Bead Cellar. Phone: 856-665-4744. Web address: www.beadcellar.com.

India silver clasp available from The Bead Cellar.

Hill Tribe silver tulip bead caps available from Tiger Tiger. Phone: 510-236-9917. Web address: www.tiger-tiger.com.

Project 3

#9 Three-cut Czech beads available from The Bead Cellar. Also available from Beyond Beadery. Phone: 303-258-9389. Web address: www.beyondbeadery.com.

Swarovski crystals available from Jane's Fiber & Beads. Phone: 888-497-2665. Web address: www.janesfiberandbeads.com. Also available from Beyond Beadery.

Winterglass beads available from Jonathan Winter (bead artist). Phone: 352-219-9053. E-mail address: winterglas1@yahoo.com.

Project 4

All items listed above.

Project 5

#11 seed beads available from Jane's Fiber & Beads.

Project 6

Paula Radke bead available from Paula Radke. Phone: 800-341-4945. Web address: www.paularadke.com.

Project 7

All items listed above.

Project 8

Hill Tribe silver spacers available from Tiger Tiger. Turkish flower spacers available from Singaraja. Flowers also available from The Bead Goes On. Phone: 508-693-7618. Web address: www.beadgoeson.com.

Bali cones available from Anil Kumar. Phone: 510-498-8455. Address: PO Box 3471, Fremont, CA, and from Singaraja.

Project 9

Clasp available from Rishashay.

Project 10

Focal beads are made by Darcy Restemayer of Silver Cloud Trading Co. Phone: 360-598-2967. Address: P.O. Box 63, Suquamish, WA 98392.

Project 11

Clasp available from Scottsdale Bead Supply. Phone: 480-945-5988. Web address: www.scottsdalebeadsupply.com.

Lampwork beads by Kathy Perras/ItzArt. Phone: 503-331-2524. Web address: www.kathyperras.com.

Project 12

Lampwork bead by Nancy Tobey. Phone: 978-772-3317. Web address: www.nancytobey.com.

Project 13(A)

Matsuno beads available from Jane's Fiber & Beads.

Clasp available from Star's Clasps. Phone: 703-938-7018. Web address: www.starsclasps.com.

Project 13(B)

All items listed above.

Project 14

All items listed above.

Project 15

All items listed above.